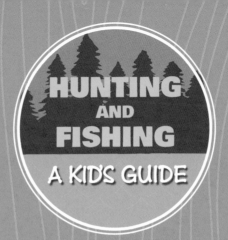

HUNTING
AND
FISHING

A KID'S GUIDE

We're Going
BIG-GAME
HUNTING

Andrew Law

PowerKiDS
press.

New York

Published in 2017 by The Rosen Publishing Group, Inc.
29 East 21st Street, New York, NY 10010

First Edition

Editor: Melissa Raé Shofner
Book Design: Tanya Dellaccio

Photo Credits: Cover Mark Raycroft/Minden Pictures/Getty Images; all pages (wood texture) sittipong/Shutterstock.com; back cover, pp. 1, 3–4, 6–8, 10, 12, 14–16, 18–20, 22, 24, 26–28, 30–32 (background) ArtBitz/Shutterstock.com; p. 4 https://commons.wikimedia.org/wiki/File:Bear_hunting_Kodiak_FWS.jpg; p. 5 Witold Skrypczak/Getty Images; p. 7 (pronghorn) KGrif/Shutterstock.com; p. 7 (mountain goat) C_Gara/Shutterstock.com; p. 7 (peccary) Dennis W. Donohue/ Shutterstock.com; p. 8 Josef Pittner/Shutterstock.com; p. 9 Christopher Gardiner/Shutterstock.com; p. 10 Claudia Paulussen/ Shutterstock.com; p. 11 Anh Luu/Shutterstock.com; p. 13 John Patriquin/Portland Press Herald/Getty Images; pp. 15 (hunter), 29 Nate Allred/Shutterstock.com; p. 15 (elk) Wesley Aston/Shutterstock.com; pp. 15 (moose), 21 Tom Tietz/ Shutterstock.com; p. 17 Hans Berggren/Getty Images; p. 19 (top) Marcel Jancovic/Shutterstock.com; p. 19 (bottom) Perry Mastrovito/Getty Images; p. 20 Lyubov_Nazarova/Shutterstock.com; p. 22 Keith Bell/Shutterstock.com; p. 23 Jeffrey B. Banke/Shutterstock.com; p. 25 Johner Images/Getty Images; p. 27 (elk cow) Doyne and Margaret Loyd/ Shutterstock.com; p. 27 (elk bull) David Osborn/Shutterstock.com; p. 30 Craig Moore/Shutterstock.com.

Cataloging-in-Publication Data

Names: Law, Andrew.
Title: We're going big-game hunting / Andrew Law.
Description: New York : PowerKids Press, 2017. | Series: Hunting and fishing: a kid's guide | Includes index.
Identifiers: ISBN 9781499427516 (pbk.) | ISBN 9781499428742 (library bound) | ISBN 9781508152798 (6 pack)
Subjects: LCSH: Big game hunting–Juvenile literature.
Classification: LCC SK35.5 L39 2017 | DDC 799.2'6–d23

Manufactured in the United States of America

CPSIA Compliance Information: Batch Batch #BW17PK: For Further Information contact Rosen Publishing, New York, New York at 1-800-237-9932

CONTENTS

A NOTE TO READERS

Always talk with a parent or teacher before proceeding with any of the activities found in this book. Some activities require adult supervision.

A NOTE TO PARENTS AND TEACHERS

This book was written to be informative and entertaining. Some of the activities in this book require adult supervision. Please talk with your child or student before allowing them to proceed with any hunting activities. The author and publisher specifically disclaim any liability for injury or damages that may result from use of information in this book.

A LONG HISTORY

Humans have been hunting large animals for thousands of years. In the past, humans depended on big-game hunting for survival. A successful hunt can still mean the difference between life and death in some parts of the world. A single animal can feed many people. Skins and furs are used to make clothes. **Antlers** can be crafted into tools.

Today, big-game hunting is usually considered a sport in much of the world. Many Americans enjoy hunting large, **dangerous** animals.

HUNTING HINT

Many big-game hunters like to show off their skills by displaying **trophies** of their kills. This bear's head was likely stuffed and displayed on a wall in the 1950s.

Newspaper Rock in Utah is covered with pictures that are more than 2,000 years old. These ancient pictures show people hunting deer, bison, and pronghorn antelope.

WHAT IS "BIG GAME"?

Many kinds of animals are hunted in the United States. Figuring out which animals are "big game" is pretty easy. Large, wild animals such as bears, moose, and elk are often considered big game. These big animals are hunted for sport. However, keep in mind that hunting laws differ from state to state. Each state has a different list of big-game animals. Alaska permits the hunting of wolves. In Florida, you can hunt alligators!

HUNTING HINT

For more information about what big-game animals can be hunted in your area, visit your state's wildlife department website.

pronghorn

mountain goat

peccary

Here are some of the big-game animals that can be hunted in the United States.

WHERE AND WHEN TO HUNT

Knowing what big-game animals to hunt is just as important as knowing where and when to hunt them. While big game is found across North America, certain animals are more common in certain areas. Moose are often found in Maine and Alaska. Pennsylvania and Montana have a large number of black bears.

Big game can only be hunted during certain times of the year. This time frame is called "open season" and is different for each animal and state. Hunting can also be limited to certain times of day.

black bear

Bighorn sheep can be hunted during the late fall in North Dakota.

HUNTING HINT

There are age limits for hunters and only a certain number of permits are given out each year. Make sure to check the rules for your state.

OBSERVING POPULATIONS

Scientists closely study animal populations. Their findings are used to decide how many animals can be hunted in an area each season. If a population is too large, more hunting may be allowed.

In the past, some big-game animals were nearly hunted into **extinction**. These days, the United States has laws to **protect** wildlife. Many of these laws exist thanks to hunters such as President Theodore Roosevelt. In other parts of the world, big-game animals such as tigers and elephants are **endangered** because hunters disobey the laws.

HUNTING HINT

If you see an animal with babies, don't shoot! It's against the law in many places.

In the 1800s, American bison were hunted to near extinction. With populations growing again, a small number of bison can be hunted each year in states such as Montana.

GETTING READY TO HUNT

Before hunting big game, you need to complete a hunting safety course. Your local sporting and outdoors clubs may offer one. The course will teach you important lessons about firearm, or gun, safety.

You also need to get a hunting **license**. This license proves that you're a **legal** hunter in your state. The legal hunting age is usually 12, but laws are different from state to state. A licensed adult may need to hunt with you until you reach a certain age.

HUNTING HINT

Groups such as the Boy Scouts of America and the National Rifle Association have more information about firearm safety on their websites.

The **minimum** hunting age in Maine used to be 10, but this changed in 2016. Maine is now one of 40 states that allow kids of any age to hunt as long as a licensed adult is with them.

WHAT TO WEAR

Big-game animals such as moose and elk are in season during chilly parts of the year. Wearing layers, or pieces of clothing over each other, will help keep you warm. You should also wear gloves that allow your fingers to move and thick socks to keep your feet warm.

Many states require hunters to wear bright orange, also called hunter orange or blaze orange. Many animals can't see hunter orange, but it's very easy for humans to see. Wearing orange will help keep you and other hunters safe while hunting big game.

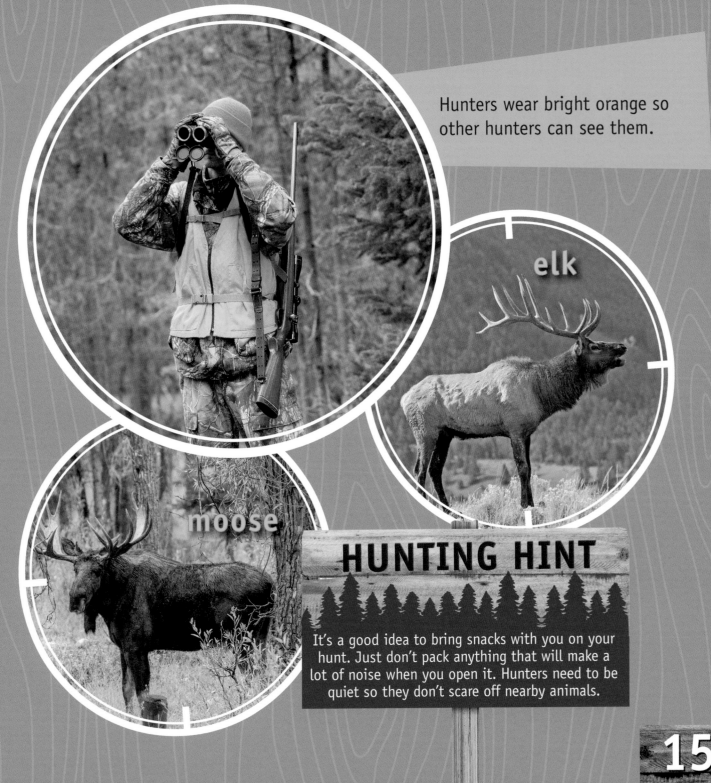

Hunters wear bright orange so other hunters can see them.

elk

moose

HUNTING HINT

It's a good idea to bring snacks with you on your hunt. Just don't pack anything that will make a lot of noise when you open it. Hunters need to be quiet so they don't scare off nearby animals.

RIFLE HUNTING

Many big-game hunters hunt with firearms. It's important to use the right gun. You wouldn't want to hunt a bear with a gun used for hunting ducks! Learning how to aim a rifle is easy.

If you decide to hunt big game with a firearm, you'll need a big rifle and the correct ammunition, or bullets. Using smaller guns to hunt big game is often illegal because these guns are less likely to kill big-game animals. It's better for animals to be killed cleanly than for them to be wounded and in pain.

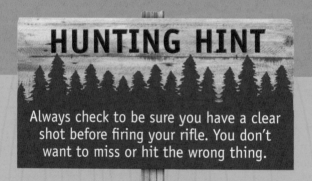

HUNTING HINT

Always check to be sure you have a clear shot before firing your rifle. You don't want to miss or hit the wrong thing.

This young woman is learning to shoot a rifle with a scope. A scope is a tool that lets a hunter see a faraway object, such as an animal, close up.

17

BOWHUNTING

Big-game hunters can also use bows. Bowhunting is harder than using a rifle because hunters have to get much closer to the animal. Since it takes some time to set up and aim an arrow, hunters also need to make their shot count.

The compound bow is popular in the United States. This bow uses cables and **pulleys** that make it easier to pull back an arrow. Some states also permit crossbow hunting. Crossbows look like a combination of a gun and a bow and are very powerful.

HUNTING HINT

Animals have a great sense of smell. Special sprays are available to help mask your human scent.

Just like hunting with a firearm, bowhunting requires a license.

LEARNING TO TRACK

The more you hunt, the better you'll get at seeing and hearing animals in the woods. You'll also get better at being quiet. Big-game animals might not look very fast because of their size, but they're quick. If they hear you, they'll most likely run.

Bowhunters must be good trackers. It's unusual for an arrow to kill big game instantly. Most animals will run away, and it may take them a while to die. Bowhunters must follow an animal's trail, sometimes for several miles.

HUNTING HINT

Before you hunt in an area, get to know it by going for walks there. Look for signs of animals and good spots for hunting.

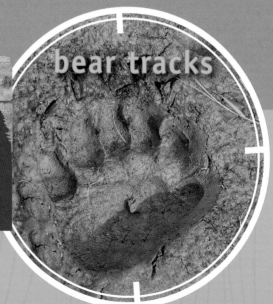

bear tracks

Hunters need to be smart to sneak up on pronghorn. They're the fastest land animals in North America, and they have great eyesight.

HUNTING METHODS

Some hunters sit quietly in one spot for several hours. They often hunt from tree stands. These are tiny elevated buildings or decks that offer excellent views of the area.

Other hunters **stalk** the animals they're hunting. They must be able to recognize tracks and walk silently through the woods. Both kinds of hunting can be combined when two or more hunters are working together. One hunter can walk around and herd animals into the open so that another hunter in a tree stand has a shot.

HUNTING HINT

Some hunters use trail cameras to record the animals that pass by. This lets hunters know which kinds of game are in an area and helps them pick a good hunting spot.

A big-game hunter sits quietly in a tree stand, waiting for an animal to appear.

23

CLEANING AND TAGGING

After making a kill, big-game hunters need to remove the animal's organs. This is called field dressing, or cleaning, the animal. It's important to do this right away so the meat doesn't spoil. Find out if there is someone in your area who can prepare the meat from your kill.

The next step is to tag the animal. A tag is a form that's usually found on your hunting license. It needs to be filled out with information such as the date and time of day. Your state's wildlife department uses this information to record how many animals have been killed.

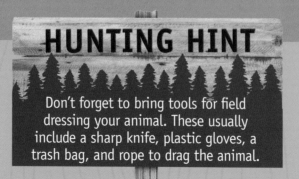

HUNTING HINT

Don't forget to bring tools for field dressing your animal. These usually include a sharp knife, plastic gloves, a trash bag, and rope to drag the animal.

Big-game animals are heavy. You might need some help dragging your kill out of the woods.

FOLLOWING THE RULES

Hunters should know and follow their state's hunting laws. These laws exist to protect animal populations. It's important to only hunt big-game animals that are in season. When hunting elk or moose, make sure you see antlers before you shoot. It's usually illegal to kill females.

Breaking a hunting law can mean an expensive fine or even the loss of your license. Breaking hunting laws on purpose is called poaching. Examples of poaching include killing more than your limit and hunting animals out of season.

HUNTING HINT

Poachers aren't respected because they don't hunt fairly. Hunting is a sport, after all. It's important that the animal gets a sporting chance.

cow

bull

A male elk has large antlers and is called a bull. A female elk is called a cow.

BIG REWARDS

Big-game hunting can be a **rewarding** activity. After making a big kill, hunters often have their picture taken. Some even have trophies, like mounts or rugs, made from their animals. Enjoying the meat is one of the most satisfying parts of hunting. Hunters also get to visit many beautiful places.

Some people are not comfortable with the fact that animals are killed for sport. However, good hunters respect wildlife. Many hunters are **environmentalists**. It's important for them to protect animals and wild places.

HUNTING HINT

Big-game hunting requires hunters to be very quiet, calm, and still for long periods of time. The rewards are worth it, though. A big kill is something to be proud of, as long as it's legal.

Big-game hunters, like this father and son, get to spend time together and enjoy nature.

MASTERING THE HUNT

It can take a lifetime to master big-game hunting. This is because the only way to learn about it is by doing it. Young people interested in hunting can get started at an early age with an adult's help.

Big-game hunting provides people with a chance to reconnect with the natural world and with the past. It's been a part of North American history for thousands of years. Big-game hunting will remain a popular sport as long as people continue to respect wildlife and enjoy nature.

GLOSSARY

antlers: The pair of horns on a deer, moose, or elk.

dangerous: Not safe.

endangered: In danger of dying out.

environmentalist: Someone working to preserve, restore, and improve the natural world.

extinction: The state of being extinct, or no longer existing.

legal: Allowed by the law.

license: An official paper giving someone the right to do something.

minimum: The lowest possible number of something.

protect: To keep safe.

pulley: A wheel or set of wheels used with a rope or chain to lift or lower heavy objects.

rewarding: Satisfying or enjoyable.

stalk: To follow something closely and secretly.

trophy: An object that can be displayed to show one's skill or success.

INDEX

WEBSITES

Due to the changing nature of Internet links, PowerKids Press has developed an online list of websites related to the subject of this book. This site is updated regularly. Please use this link to access the list: www.powerkidslinks.com/hunt/big